Nature Has Spots

Katie Peters

GRL Consultants,
Diane Craig and Monica Marx,
Certified Literacy Specialists

Pull Ahead READERS

Lerner Publications ◆ Minneapolis

Note from a GRL Consultant
This Pull Ahead leveled book has been carefully designed for beginning readers. A team of guided reading literacy experts has reviewed and leveled the book to ensure readers pull ahead and experience success.

Lerner Publications Company
A division of Lerner Publishing Group, Inc.
241 First Avenue North
Minneapolis, MN 55401 USA

For reading levels and more information, look up this title at www.lernerbooks.com.

Main body text set in Memphis Pro 24/39
Typeface provided by Linotype.

Photo Acknowledgments
The images in this book are used with the permission of: © Shutterstock (all)

Front cover: © Shutterstock

Library of Congress Cataloging-in-Publication Data

Names: Peters, Katie, author.
Title: Nature has spots / Katie Peters.
Description: Minneapolis : Lerner Publications, [2020] | Series: Science all around me (Pull ahead readers - Nonfiction) | Includes index. | Audience: Age 4–7. | Audience: K to Grade 3.
Identifiers: LCCN 2018058165 (print) | LCCN 2019000016 (ebook) | ISBN 9781541562257 (eb pdf) | ISBN 9781541558489 (lb : alk. paper) | ISBN 9781541573307 (pb : alk. paper)
Subjects: LCSH: Animals—Color—Juvenile literature.
Classification: LCC QL767 (ebook) | LCC QL767 .P477 2020 (print) | DDC 591.47—dc23

LC record available at https://lccn.loc.gov/2018058165

Manufactured in the United States of America
2-51164-46229-6/9/2021

Contents

Nature Has Spots

The leopard has spots.

The deer has spots.

The giraffe has spots.

The frog has spots.

The bug has spots.

The fish has spots.

Did You See It?

bug

deer

fish

frog

giraffe

leopard

Index